Every day You lift me up with Your angels;

*Every night You bring
me to my knees.*

*Every prayer has
been answered
because of Your power;*

*Not a detail left
undone.*

*Every day,
Lord, I
thank You . . .*

The Other Side Of The Bed

by Cookie Bannon

Illustrated by Lee Angst

Beaver's Pond Press, Inc.

Edina / Minnesota

ISBN 1-59298-045-7

Library of Congress Catalog Number: 2003114013

Cover design and illustrations by Lee Angst
Interior design by Rachel Holscher
Typesetting by Stanton Publications Services, Inc.

Printed in Canada

First Printing: December 2003

07 06 05 04 03   6 5 4 3 2 1

Beaver's Pond Press, Inc.

7104 Ohms Lane, Suite 216
Edina, MN 55439-2129
(952) 829-8818
www.BeaversPondPress.com

To order, visit www.BookHouseFulfillment.com or call
1-800-901-3480. Reseller discounts available.

Children's Hospital of Illinois
at OSF Saint Francis Medical Center

Our Mission is to improve the health status of children by providing integrated, comprehensive pediatric health care services for children from birth to 18 years of age. As a premier children's health care system, we address the spiritual, emotional, and physical needs of the pediatric patient based on three principles:

1. *Children are unique and have special needs.*

2. *A child's illness impacts the entire family.*

3. *Childhood illness interferes with normal childhood growth and development.*

For more information about Children's Hospital of Illinois
and Cookie Bannon write to:
Cookie Bannon
Children's Hospital of Illinois
530 NE Glen Oak Ave.
Peoria, IL 61637
www.childrenshospitalofil.org
309-655-2321
or
309-671-4815

On behalf of Children's Hospital of Illinois administration and staff and the families we care for each day, I want to extend my sincere gratitude to the following for their generous contributions to this project:

ANNA HEART OF ILLINOIS

  CHAPTER 319

AmerenCILCO

Appliance Distributors Incorporated
In memory of Dirk Swardenski

Ronald & Patsy Butler
In memory of Jonathon Hamilton

Carpet Weavers

Child Care Connection

Consumer Credit Counseling Service of
  Central Illinois, Inc.

Cops 4 Kids

COUNTRY.
Insurance & Financial Services

Emil & Jan Deissler
In honor of their healthy grandchildren

Paul & Teresa Dubravec and Family
In honor of Joseph Paul Dubravec

First Capital Bank

Terry & Nancy Flynn
In memory of Meghan Flynn

Heart of Illinois Association for the
  Education of Young Children

John Hancock Financial Services, Inc.

Mark & Kim Johnson and Family

David & Sharon Joseph

Kelch Floors

Norm Kelly

Knapp-Johnson Funeral Home

Phil & Barb Kuhl

ICC Child Care Connection

Dave & Regina Lavalee and Family

Limestone Walters Parents Club

Rex & Laurie Linder

Brett & Karla Lohman and Family
In memory of Lauren Lohman

Lohman Companies

Ron & Vickie McDonald

Mercer County Hospital

Mike Murphy Ford

Morton Public Library

Mark & Bridget Nelan and Family

Brad & Michelle O'Brien and Family
In memory of Molly O'Brien

Peoria Siding and Window Company

Peoria Speedway / Sherrie Hamilton
In memory of Chuck Hamilton

Saturn of Peoria

Ed & Connie Scherer
In memory of Eric Scherer

Doug & Cristi Schaffnit and Family

Rusty, Jana & Maggie Schopp
In memory of Eric Schopp

Sheet Metal Products Company

St. Ann's Catholic Church

St. Matthew Altar and Rosary

St. Monica Guild

St. Patrick's Altar and Rosary Society

St. Paul's Lutheran Church

St. Peter's Lutheran Church

Mr. & Mrs. Joel Storm and Family

Mr. & Mrs. Joseph R. Stowell, Jr.
In memory of Joey Stowell, III

The Digital Store—Trivalent
Communications

Margaret A. Toniny

Vonachen, Lawless, Trager, Slevin
Attorneys at law

Dan & Karen Waibel and Family

To Mari, Theresa, Patsy, Gail, and Monica

*Your remarkable talents shine amidst these pages, forever reminding
me that the true gifts of one cannot be fully realized until they become
intertwined with the gifts of others. Thank you for your tireless commitment
and patience, precision, faith, encouragement, and insight. God bless you
for standing beside me on the other side of the bed.*

Dedicated to

Elaine • Kevin • Maureen

I love you

Contents

 Preface

I often wonder about the details behind the lyrics of a song. As a singer-songwriter, I can't imagine composing a piece of music that has not evolved directly from my life.

The 12 chapters in *The Other Side of the Bed* reveal the circumstances, the emotions, and the background of the songs included on the enclosed CD.

As an employee of Children's Hospital of Illinois, I have been honored to share my gift of music at the bedside of hospitalized children for more than 18 years. Creating a sense of peace and inspiring joy has been my goal. My inner desire? To lessen the anxiety that comes in the midst of an unexpected or unwanted situation.

One of my greatest lessons in life has been that adversity—no matter how challenging—is a remarkable opportunity for growth, not only for the individual experiencing it, but also for those who choose to take part in easing the pain of another.

On the morning of July 20, 2000, God lifted me up, surrounded me with love, and then—keeping His promise as the great "I Am"—He gently carried me to the other side of the bed.

John 15:13-15

Greater love has no one than this; that he lay down his life for his friends. You are my friends if you do what I command. I no longer call you servants, because a servant does not know his master's business. Instead, I have called you friends, for everything that I have learned from my Father I have made known to you.

ad's favorite line was, "I am the father of eleven children. They're all boys except ten." I am daughter #5, child #6. The youngest of the oldest, oldest of the youngest. Smack dab in the middle. Born in 1955, I was baptized Patricia Ann Bannon. Humored by the resemblance of my fat cheeks to a certain round treat, my family became accustomed to calling me "Cookie" before my first birthday.

My five older siblings, the big kids, considered me and my five younger siblings to be the little kids. I never understood their logic and yearned to be one of the big kids. Their special privileges enticed me—dating, driving, phone calls, homecomings, proms, and extended curfews with friends. I remember 1963 and my parents' trip to the World's Fair. The big kids went; the little kids stayed home. That was that! I'm still pouting.

Our family of 13 lived in a five-bedroom home. With only one bathroom, we were not allowed the privilege to pamper ourselves. Instead, sharing became a way of life: the sink, the "john," the tub, the mirror, towels, curlers, the hairdryer, and makeup; bedrooms, dressers, closets, and beds; sweaters, blouses, skirts, dresses, jeans, and shoes. Arguing erupted if a new outfit was borrowed without permission from the owner. All lending came to a halt until both parties cooled down.

My siblings and I learned the value of friendship at an early age. It was unavoidable and necessary for a peaceful household. My brother did yard work and took out the garbage; I don't recall seeing him vacuum. The rest of us entertained ourselves while doing chores—dancing in the kitchen doing dishes and polishing the hardwood floors with worn-out bath towels under our feet. The broom handle was irresistible as the limbo stick when someone was sweeping the floor. At night we set each others' hair with bobby pins and rollers, scratched each others' backs and giggled as we shared secrets in our cozy beds. My father's final instruction of the day, "Quiet up there," immediately settled the household when the giggling was out of control.

My parents spoke with one voice. They had vowed to support each other in their parenting duties, so asking Dad for permission after Mom said, "No, you can't go," was a scheme none of us could pull off, especially me. They didn't always call me Cookie. When I heard the name "Patricia," a lecture was soon to follow, along with the hours, days, or weeks I was to be grounded. Other than Mom or Dad in disciplinary mode, only one other person used my given name.

Larry insisted on calling me "Pat." He was a classmate at St. Cecilia's Grade School. Although this irritated me more than fingernails scraping a chalkboard and chewing lunch with your mouth open, I never challenged him about it, knowing his life most likely would end long before mine. Frail from head to toe, yet blessed with a heart prepared for heaven, Larry faced every day battling cystic fibrosis. Throughout grade school, his friendship unknowingly directed me toward maturity and taught me compassion.

As a young child, however, I lacked the maturity to appreciate the perpetual sacrifices my parents made. Now I realize Mom and Dad planted seeds within the depths of my heart that allowed me to grasp the meaning and value of true friendship. Giving when they had nothing to give taught me how small gestures can mean so much to others. The little white envelopes my parents placed in the collection basket every Sunday morning represented a sacrifice that was the threshold to 12 years of formal Catholic education for each of their children.

The cane belonging to my maternal grandfather, Felix Anton, figures prominently in my memories of those years. Its sole purpose was to bridge the gap between the backs of two dining room chairs. As the contents of the ironing basket slowly dwindled away, pure white, round-collared blouses, sizes 6x to 12, and many plaid uniforms, starched and ready to wear, were hung on the walking stick.

The ironing board and my most cherished piece of furniture, a three-legged oak stool with a painted red seat, were always planted nearby. When Mom wasn't sitting on the stool at the ironing board, it served as a beauticians chair. I often squirmed there as she cut my hair. I never figured out why I always had a pixie cut and my sister Ginny (daughter #6, child #7; prim, proper, rarely in trouble) was allowed to have her long blond pony tail. She always reminded me "You deserve to be grounded, Cookie!" as she passed me on the stairway, flinging her pony tail in front of my face.

Friendship prevailed, however, and our fighting never lasted long as we made our way toward St. Cecilia's every morning. Those starched white blouses and uniforms, saddle shoes, schoolbooks covered by brown paper grocery bags, pencil boxes, and book bags, combined with the priceless gift of freedom of religion, molded my siblings and me as our parents denied themselves many of life's pleasures.

"Ham salad" really consisted of a three-pound chunk of bologna. New carpeting, a new car, and color TV never made it to the top of their priority list. Every year on Saturday morning before Easter, I remember piling into the station wagon. Destination: Hills Brothers Shoes, which advertised "Two for five, man alive." Purchasing black patent-leather shoes, usually six pairs at a time, to the tune of $15 plus tax, was definitely more economical than shopping at an expensive department store.

I was too young at the time to comprehend how difficult it was for Mom and Dad to scrape together $5 every Tuesday afternoon to pay for my piano lessons. Their frugality facilitated my luxury of sitting attentively on the piano bench at Mrs. Becker's house. Unfortunately for me, I practiced watching my fingers move upon the ivory keys instead of what filled the pages of music at eye level before me. "Chopsticks" was the only song I ever mastered. To this day, I read notes by the "All cars eat gas" and "Every good boy does fine" method.

The lessons served their purpose by sparking my interest in music. During the summer between sixth and seventh grades, with the assistance of my brother Kevin (#1 and only son, child #5; patient, inventive, best brother ever), I was able to learn four guitar chords: G, Em, D, and D7. This minor triumph enabled me to sing and play Peter, Paul, and Mary's "If I Had a Hammer." Suffering from a very calloused set of left digits, I began to sense a gift, unaware of the extent to which my future would embrace this new passion. I was certain music would be a part of me forever, as would a sunny afternoon in 1972 at Peoria's Academy of Our Lady.

Mr. Bradle had procured several lifeless cats to be dissected by his hesitant biology students. Growing up in a family that preferred dogs as pets didn't prevent me from feeling deathly ill during the gruesome experience. So I used my bargaining skills, imploring the highly respected faculty member to excuse me, assuring him that I would not waste the time. His approval led me directly to my locker. Opening the door, I examined the contents of the tall gray metal closet. Along with several dried corsages, secret notes, and photographs of my cherished classmates was my Yamaha acoustic guitar.

I have no recollection where I nested that afternoon as I wrote the song "Friends." What has settled in my memory is the gratefulness that stirred within me as my hand scribbled the following phrase on the reverse side of a wrinkled English assignment: *"Friends, I love my friends . . . I love the helping hand, and the smiles they give each day."*

The music unfolded gracefully while the lyrics molded themselves one measure at a time. By the end of the hour, my first "original concerto" was complete.

I sang "Friends," sitting on the edge of the stage in the theater at the Academy of Our Lady in 1973 after my classmates and I received our class rings. One of my best friends, Mary Jo, painted the lyrics upon canvas as a gift to me before we graduated from high school. Singing "Friends" as part of the "Ring Day" ceremony became a tradition until 1980, when my baby sister Joanne (daughter #10, child #11; witty, overprotective, the only one to receive her driver's license on her sixteenth birthday) received her class ring.

As a little kid I wanted to be big. Now that I'm grown I wish being a little kid could have lasted . . . just a little longer. When I was growing up, I loved my family. Today they are my dearest friends. What a gift it is to have a friend. What an honor it is to be one.

Friends, I love my friends.
I love the helping hand
And the smiles they give each day.
Friends, I need my friends.
I need their helping hand and I need them more each day.
They are always around, especially when you're down and lonely.
They may tell a joke or sit with you for awhile.
When you need some care or you have a secret,
They're there to share it.
You always depend on them for going along with your dreams
And setting up your schemes.
Friends, I want my friends around.
You know how good it is to have them there.

Friends, sometimes they let you down,
But, then they come around to show you that they care.
If you need a friend, just take my hand and I'll smile for you,
Smile for you, my friend.
If you need a friend, just hold my hand and I'll walk with you;
l love you my friend.
If you need a friend, just take my hand and I'll smile for you,
Smile for you my friend.
If you need a friend, take my hand and I'll walk with you;
l love you. I love you. I'll love you my friend.
Always my friend.

Isaiah 6:8

Then I heard the Lord's voice, saying, 'Whom can I send? Who will go for us?' So I said, 'Here I am. Send me!'

s I sat opposite her desk, I crossed my legs, left over right, right over left—fidgeting like a first-grader waiting for permission to go potty. She was just outside the door, conversing with a colleague. Scanning her office, I was intrigued by the framed diplomas hung carefully on the walls. My hands were beginning to sweat, reminiscent of the days of my youth when

- I got caught talking to a boy on the telephone, then tried to convince Mom it was my best girlfriend's little brother asking for help with his math. Busted: I didn't even like math.
- I broke my mother's antique blue hobnail-glass perfume bottle, hid the remains at the bottom of the garbage can, then blamed my little sister

Jean Marie (daughter #9, child #10; astute, stunning, best back-scratcher ever) when Mom discovered it was missing off her dresser. Grounded: Jean wasn't tall enough to reach the top of that chest of drawers.
- On Christmas morning 1967, a shiny white octagonal box with a gold lid tempted me. It waited on the floor at

the foot of my parents' bed for me to peek inside. My dad was snoring on the bed, or so I thought. When I saw the burgundy velvet hat with tassels hanging over the side like a graduation cap, I prayed the hat was for anyone but me. Maybe my sister Barb (daughter #3, child #3; logical, mischievous, naïve in a delightful way). I hoped if it was a gift for her she could find it in her heart to graciously accept the ugliest Christmas present ever. One hour before midnight Mass, Dad and Mom gave me an early gift. Humiliated: I looked like the youngest member of the Mohammed Shrine Temple!

The daydreaming stopped as the ants in my pants returned. To the best of my knowledge, I had been following the rules. My first year working in pediatrics as an activity therapy assistant had proven to be a success, according to my recent evaluation. So why was I wringing my clammy hands, and then biting a nail or two? Why did I feel as if my deodorant was failing?

She had approached me at the nurses station in pediatrics. My discussion with the unit clerk at the front desk ended abruptly when "Mrs. D." tapped me on the shoulder. Turning suddenly, I met her face to face. Without so much as a smile, she looked directly into my eyes, saying, "Cookie, I want to see you in my office."

Joyce Dougherty had been the supervisor on the children's unit since 1973. Some would describe her as a drill sergeant, always determined to run a tight ship with high expectations from her staff. This woman had little tolerance for anything less than perfect.

Again, thoughts ricocheted in my head: *Had I made too much noise with Jesse Camp in his room that morning? It wasn't my fault that the five-year-old's laughter echoed beyond the walls of his room as we played hide-and-seek.*

Jesse chose his closet for a hiding place. Playing along, I called out, "Jesse, where are you?" He found it hysterical that I couldn't locate him. It never occurred to Jesse that the tube providing air to his nostrils was the same plastic hose slithering underneath the closet door, trailing across the room, and attached to the oxygen tank next to his bed. This experienced activity therapist had no intention of bursting his bubble.

Anyway, it was worth losing the game just to watch Jesse throw open the door of the closet and hear him screech with laughter, "Give up, Cookie! Give up! Give in, I win! You couldn't find me!"

Jesse's spirit never missed the chance to thaw a cold heart. Battling the ravages of cystic fibrosis seemed to be the least of his concerns. Even Mrs. D. couldn't resist his charm. The personality of "Private Jesse Camp" never ceased to subdue the demands of the "drill sergeant."

She was still yacking out in the hall. The what-ifs continued to nag at me. I was restless, wondering if I had violated patient confidentiality. Maybe I hadn't divided my time equally among the patients. I waited for my sentencing. Finally, she entered her office.

Her words surprised me. "I have an idea. In fact, the idea is so wonderful I woke my husband up in the middle of the night to tell him about it." My hands were saturated. She continued, "You have been an employee in pediatrics for over a year now. Our first Children's Miracle Network Telethon is less than a month away. I think you should write a song about the children we care for each day. I want you to write lyrics and the music, and then sing it on TV. You can do this, I know it! You have just a little more than three weeks, so you'd better start today. Come sing it for me when you're finished."

I bargained with her, insisting the project was impossible, suggesting, "Maybe next year," adding, "I've only written one song. That was back in high school 13 years ago! I don't know where to start."

"From your heart," she replied, with an unforgettable twinkle in her eyes.

As I left her office, my heart carried me back to those high school days. I remembered keeping perfect time to the band Chicago's "25 or 6 to 4" as a pom-pom girl and singing every word along with Don McLean and my best friends while playing "American Pie" full blast on the radio. Cat Stevens' "Tea For The Tillerman" held first place as my favorite album. "Teach Your Children" by Crosby, Stills, Nash & Young was a favorite song. Yet folk music appealed to me due to the fact that my guitar-playing was limited.

I would find a quiet place to sing and perfect the chord progression of a simple melody. Little did I know as a teenager that learning to sing and play the music for "Puff The Magic Dragon" and "The Marvelous Little Toy" would be God's first tap on my shoulder, directing me toward my future with children.

After graduating from high school, I registered at Peoria's local community college with the desire to become an occupational therapist. As a young student, I vacillated between the importance of my education and the fantasy that being married and having children would be my key to paradise. In April 1975, after completing only one semester of college, I forfeited my bachelor's degree for a marriage license.

Seeking a job, I filled out an application at OSF Saint Francis Medical Center, Peoria, Illinois. Two small boxes in the lower right-hand corner of the application followed the question, "Do you have any talents?" The question intrigued me. Instantly, I considered my music interests and abilities, thinking, *Sure, I have talents.* I penciled in the box under the "yes" column with a strong sense of assurance the answer could be my chance for a future in health care. So I wrote this comment in small letters: "I play the guitar and sing . . . a little." Those seven words changed my life forever.

I was hired full time as an activity therapy assistant. My specific duties were to provide activities for adults in the rehabilitation unit. Those patients and their families opened my eyes to a brand-new outlook on life. For the first time,

I was faced with the heart-wrenching pain that comes from observing people who are dealing with adversity.

Although music was not part of my job description, I took my guitar to the hospital several times a week that first year. Typically, I sang for rehabilitation patients confined to their room and at birthday celebrations and holiday parties. When the census was low, however, I would venture beyond the rehabilitation unit to seek someone in need of a song. A doctor caught on to my out-of-bounds mission.

While thinking about the early days of my work at OSF Saint Francis, I realized I had a title for the song Mrs. D. wanted me to write: "Miracle Child." It occurred to me I had been present in the midst of a miracle ten years earlier, when the pediatrician stopped me in the hall. His last words as he directed me to his patient's room were, "Cookie, your music may bring some comfort to the family as they wait by his bedside."

The little boy's name was Robert. I clearly recall introducing myself as Cookie. Robert's mom and dad chuckled as most people do when they hear my name. Looking at their son, one would never know this beautiful boy was so distant from the world. He had been comatose for five months. Robert's parents welcomed me as they shared his story. Being 21 and not yet a parent myself, I could not empathize with them. However, the fact that I had come from a large family enabled me to sympathize with the notion, "There but for the grace of God go I."

Within minutes, I knew of their son's favorite pastime: raising rabbits. It was his grade school picture taped to the wall above his bed that captured my heart. The photo revealed his sparkling brown eyes and a magnified saintly smile. I gazed upon the motionless child surrounded by a metal railing. Reminding me of Bambi, his eyelashes were dark and long, the kind every woman yearns for.

I asked Robert's mom, "What is this little guy's favorite song?" *Why did I ask that? What if I don't know it?*

As my doubts surfaced, our eyes met, and she responded with hope in her eyes, " 'Puff The Magic Dragon.' That's his favorite."

Softly a prayer escaped my heart. *Thank you, Lord, I know this one.* My fingers began to pick the strings of my guitar as the music told the story of a boy and his imaginary friend. As I finished the final note, Robert's mom whispered softly, "He used to pick up the needle on the Peter, Paul, and Mary album to play his favorite song over and over again. Could you sing it one more time?"

I honored her sweet request. Then in the middle of the song, just about when "Jackie Paper" ceases to return, Robert's huge brown eyes opened, scanning his hospital room. "Hi, Mom," he whispered. The room erupted with emotion!

Overflowing with memories of Robert, I focused on the task of writing a song. The song Mrs. Dougherty was so sure I could compose for the telethon seemed to be trapped as I scratched and scribbled words, crumpled paper, and ripped it to pieces. The next 12 days left me at an unsuccessful drawing board. Nothing seemed good enough. Every line seemed "cheesy," insincere, too poetic or unrealistic.

Then, late Friday afternoon one week prior to the telethon, I watched my coworker calm an agitated child. The little girl was thrashing back and forth, sitting up, lying down, kicking, screaming, and hitting because she didn't want a shot. With the ease of angel wings, Terri gathered the child in her arms. It was like watching the energy of a grasshopper transform to the serenity of a ladybug.

Terri and I shared the responsibilities of the pediatric activity room. Her laugh was infectious, her appearance, meticulous. She coordinated eye shadow with hair accessories that complemented her shoes, which matched her outfit. Imagination was her forte, unfolding each day as she turned child's play into healing. By her example of creativity and gentleness, she became my mentor. Terri embraced life one moment at a time, thriving on the promise of God's love.

So, combined with the enthusiasm of the delightful Mrs. Dougherty, and with my heart inspired by memories of Robert and the gentleness of Terri, "Miracle Child" was born. Ironically, Robert was one of the "miracle kids" that year. His miracle was proclaimed through a television interview with his parents. Ten years had evaporated, and his eyelashes were still just as beautiful.

The song debuted in Mrs. Dougherty's office. To my surprise, one week later, I sang it in front of the cameras on the first local telecast of the Children's Miracle Network Telethon, June 1,1986, with a smile and a tear. I didn't even fidget like a first-grader!

We care for you. We try to understand.

There is someone special here, to hold onto your little hand,

When you feel afraid, when you're crying,

When you're lying there alone, missing Mom and Dad and your own home.

We'll sing you songs about "Puff The Magic Dragon,"

A" Marvelous Little Toy" and the man in the moon.

And when you're feeling blue, we'll talk to you and make you smile again.

We want to be your friend, and make you feel at home.

We'll peek in on you to see if you're OK.

We'll tuck you in at night,

Tomorrow's going to be a better day.

Sometimes you'll find we'll hold you very tight.
You're innocent, you're lovable, you're heaven sent, you're a miracle.
A miracle.
A miracle child.

In memory of:

Terri Sherwood

March 26, 1962–February 28, 1993

and

Jesse Camp

December 11, 1980–August 23, 1988

Matthew 18:3,4

And He said: 'I tell you the truth, unless you change and become like little children, you will never enter the kingdom of heaven. Therefore, whoever humbles himself like this child is the greatest in the kingdom of heaven.'

y day had begun earlier than usual. While enthusiastically approaching the activity therapy room, purse and jacket in hand, I was distracted. A multicolored plaid cotton curtain provided privacy in room G215 in the pediatrics unit. Commotion on the other side stopped me. I alerted the occupants of the hospital room by knocking faintly on the doorway, then entered with caution. Peeking beyond the barrier, my eyes focused upon a five-year-old sitting on the bed. Tyler. I contemplated his innocence as he vomited relentlessly.

Immediately I dampened a washcloth with cool water for his hot, though adorable, face. Not too cold, not too hot, not too wet—folded just right. Comforting the little guy was my goal. Holding the cloth gently against his forehead, I began singing "Jesus Loves Me." Music and moisture did not qualify as a rescue team. Tyler spoke and threw up in one swift breath, declaring, "Not dat one, Cookie."

Consumed with a momentary desire to giggle, I shrugged my shoulders in a so-sorry-to-disappoint-you gesture. The small-town boy raised his eyebrows at me. I reckoned I'd better come up with a solution that would satisfy him immediately. It was my purpose there, and he knew it. Assured of my choice and aware of his love for his grandfather's farm, I began singing, "Old MacDonald had a farm Ee i ee io."

To my surprise, Tyler rebelled a second time and vetoed my selection. "Not dat one eiver, Cook. How 'bout you sing dat 'Puff the Magic Dwagon' for me?"

Quickly, I began singing about Jackie Paper and his imaginary friend. Obviously, a cappella was not a form of music Tyler had grown to appreciate. The degree of Tyler's discontentment was clear. In his opinion, I had failed again. He blasted the emesis basin one last time, looked up with his watery eyes and demanded, "Go get your guitar!"

So off I went to trade my belongings for the instrument. As I lifted it out of the case, a gentle peace brushed my heart. *God chose me to be surrounded by little children who face their days dealing with the unexpected, who in turn expect me to "make it better" with a song.* I headed back to Tyler's room.

Cast upon my back was the leather guitar strap, tooled with the words "Children's Hospital of Illinois," painted in primary colors. The six-string was in perfect tune. As I sang "Puff" sitting at the foot of Tyler's bed, I remembered how I felt as a child after a bout with nausea. I was relieved for him. Tears trickled like subtle drops of rain from his eyes, disappearing like magic as they saturated the fabric of his blue and yellow "Daffy Duck" hospital gown. Seeing his dimples deep as canyons and his smile rejuvenated, I discovered the reward of being in the right place at the right time.

Challenging me that morning was one determined child. One, who in the midst of feeling so miserable, still had the motivation to express what he wanted. He couldn't control the battle between his belly and his breakfast. What he could control was the person who provided a unique remedy following his surrender.

Tyler taught me to recognize the child within me that day. To play more, worry less. To appreciate what is freely given, and respect the ability to give freely. To speak simply, yet with conviction. To be strong, to smile, to dream, and never deny myself the promise of hope.

That evening, after reflecting on the lessons from Tyler, I wrote the lyrics to "More Like Children." The following morning, I sang the unpolished version for him. He proclaimed it "The song you wrote for me after I frew up."

Gather your thoughts. Forget about your fears.
Reminisce a moment about your childhood years.
Reflect upon those memories you hold deep in your soul,
And dream for just a minute that you're not very old.

I believe if we thought more like children,
We would find it so easy to care.
And the gifts that are free—fields of flowers and the trees—
Would remain in our mind and live there.
And God's gifts that are free:
Gentle rain, sun and the sea,
Would prevail in our hearts and live there.

I believe if we spoke more like children,
If our language once again became simple and sweet.
Saying, "I love you too. I'll do that for you."
"Please," now and then, "Would you like to be my friend?"
Oh, if we only spoke more like children,

Precious words are so easy to share.

Oh, if we only hoped more like children.
If the dreams in our hearts all came true.
We would smile through our tears.
Our strength would outweigh our fears.
There's such joy in what they give.
Oh, if we could only live more like children.
We would smile through our tears.
Our strength would outweigh our fears.
There's such joy in what they give.
Oh, if we could only live more like children.
Oh, if we could only love more like children.

For Tyler

Jeremiah 1:5

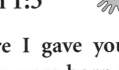

I chose you before I gave you life, and before you were born I selected you to be a prophet to the nations.

orking for women who pray for their employees every single day is quite an honor. It's a joy to be respected for the effort I put forth in my work. What a privilege to have a job in an institution where the mission is to "Nurse the sick with the greatest care and love," knowing you're acknowledged, appreciated, even admired, as a child of God.

Although The Sisters of the Third Order of St. Francis had provided care for children over the decades, a higher level of sophistication in pediatric services was attained with the establishment of Children's Hospital of Illinois early in 1990. Like many children's hospitals throughout the country, Children's Hospital of Illinois became a vital new hospital within the walls of a larger institution—in this case, OSF Saint Francis Medical Center.

At a committee meeting that had been convened to select a mascot for Children's Hospital of Illinois, someone mentioned a walking, talking, singing employee who could proclaim to the public the "mission for this hospital within a hospital" on a full-time basis. That employee happened to be me. Granted, I walked, talked, and sang every day. In fact, I loved my job and, frankly, my career couldn't

have been better at the time. The position appeared to be a promotion, but I didn't exactly jump at the opportunity.

After six years working as an activity therapy assistant in pediatrics, my colleagues recognized a talent within me that I had not yet discovered. In their eyes, it was evident that my talents had developed beyond the boundaries that I had established. They encouraged me to accept this new position and its formal recognition of my two roles: In addition to singing in our general pediatric unit, my music could bring comfort at the bedside of fragile infants in neonatal intensive care and children fighting for their lives in pediatric intensive care. Sharing the story and the mission of Children's Hospital of Illinois throughout the community would be the secondary focus.

The offer intrigued me, but I struggled with the notion of dividing my time between my patients and the community. Most of the time it was fun spending my days in pediatrics. When it wasn't, the learning experiences were immeasurable, rewarding, and enlightening. I don't mean for this to sound harsh, but most adults wail and whine more on a perfect day than any sick child does in the hospital, and even more than a dying child on his or her last day. As difficult as some situations were, they were moments that have molded me. So my supervisor and I bargained. I'd take a chance and dedicate one year to the "mascot" idea with one stipulation: I would never be required to wear an inflatable "Cookie costume."

My first presentation was a trial run. It took place in a small conference room, standing before several Children's Hospital managers and some of my peers. Despite what the experts say, imagining them in birthday suits was not a solution to calm my fears. Capturing the childlike sparkle in their eyes, however, enabled me to maintain my composure. As a result, administrative cheerleaders christened me with the title of my life: community representative for Children's Hospital of Illinois at OSF Saint Francis Medical Center. With a title like that, it seems as if some letters should come after my name, like MD, PhD or MSW.

I am humbled to count as my "credentials" the letters that form the names of children who have blessed my life. They almost outnumber the stars. It would take volumes to name every child who carried a piece of my heart with them as they went home to their earthly house, or the home sheltering them for eternity, in the arms of God.

With a combination of anxiety and determination, I began a journey outside my comfort zone. As my public performances increased, it was apparent God had prepared me to share the stories about the miracles He still performs every day.

As it has been said, "God equips the called; He does not call the equipped." God knew back in 1984 that I would eventually become the Children's Hospital community representative. When my former supervisor from OSF Saint Francis Medical Center called to ask if I would be interested in a part-time position, it may have been her voice I heard, but now I know it was God calling. I was on my knees in my living room, praying, "Lord, I can't do this anymore," the moment my telephone rang.

My children, Elaine, Kevin, and Maureen, were born in 1977, 1978, and 1979 respectively. After Kevin was born, I quit my job in rehabilitation at OSF, then began providing day care in my home for extra income. Those days were packed with activity, especially the following year when Maureen arrived. I wouldn't trade that time for anything. Those were some of the sweetest days of my life.

By the time my children were four, five, and six, my marriage had failed. Being single with three little ones of my own and five other children entrusted to my care every day, I began to feel a yearning in my heart. I missed the camaraderie I had established through my coworkers and former patients. So when the opportunity was offered to spend twenty hours a week working with adult patients, this babysitter hired a babysitter!

God clearly provided me with all I needed to serve Him, one experience at a time. I started back with OSF on July 9, 1984. Sharing my talents with adult patients in the outpatient dialysis unit was gratifying. What I gained from my experience there was far more than anything I could have ever given. My patients went through hell to stay alive, yet taught me to treasure the gift of good health.

Eight months later, a phone call came from my boss, informing me, "One of our pediatric activity therapists is ill. She is going on a leave of absence. I need you to cover her area for ten days until I can figure out what else to do. Meet me at eight o'clock tomorrow morning so I can introduce you to the staff."

I responded in a panic, "I can't relate to little hospitalized kids. God wants me here with adults. I took this job to get away from little people during the day. These patients relax me. I go home and enjoy my own children every night. These patients need me, and I don't want to disappoint them. Can't you find someone else to do this?" Then I took a breath.

I listened as she said firmly, "Ten days, Cookie, that's what I need from you. I know you; I'm sure you can do this. I'll see you in the morning." Click.

Indeed, God equips the called. It has been a magnificent "ten days." He called me by name. By answering "yes," I have been blessed abundantly. His answer to my prayer, as I knelt in my living room, was His opportunity to choose the future "community representative for Children's Hospital of Illinois at OSF Saint Francis Medical Center." It was His way of blessing me with my "Master's" degree.

He called me by name. Into my heart He came.
He has reached out for me. His grace, He gives it freely.
He called me. He called me by name.

Let go of all fear. See, the Lord is here now.
Let Him wrap His arms around you. It is He that surrounds you.
He calls you. He calls you by name.

Let Him in your heart. Let Him be the only one.
Count on Him for everything. Love Him; that's all He asks.
He calls me. He calls me by name.

He called me by name. Into my heart He came.
He has reached out for me. His grace, He gives it freely.
He called me. He called me by name.

Let Him in your heart. Let him be the only one.
Count on Him for everything. Love Him; that is all He asks.

Let Him in your heart. Count on Him for everything.
Love Him; that is all He asks.

He called me.
He called you.
He calls us by name.

In honor of:
The Sisters of the Third Order of St. Francis

1 John 4: 7-10

Dear friends, we should love each other, because love comes from God. Everyone who loves has become God's child and knows God. Whoever does not love does not know God, because God is love. This is what real love is: It is not our love for God; it is God's love for us in sending His Son to be the way to take away our sins.

atisfying the hunger pangs of his children with one pound of hamburger, a large onion, two pounds of macaroni, and 46 ounces of tomato juice was a breeze for my dad. Sprinkled with a lot of pepper, his "quick spaghetti" simmering on the stove was my first clue that Mom was going shopping or to a meeting for the evening. He usually made a huge batch of chili on Saturdays between the brisk and bitter months of September and February. There were rarely leftovers. I would bet nine out of his eleven children spread mayonnaise on the lettuce, not the bread. I try to forget his lumpy oatmeal on cold winter mornings. I will never forget how high he could push me on a swing, run underneath it, then laugh with me from the other side.

Every once in awhile—because he could—he listened in on the phone calls of his teenage daughters. My father didn't use foul language, and if a boyfriend of one of his daughter's did, the courtship was over. Drive-in theaters, R-rated movies, soap operas, and *Peyton Place* were forbidden. Wearing too much eye makeup, slamming doors, saying "shut-up," and talking back to our mother were unacceptable.

At least once a day, Dad made a trip to the grocery store for Mom. He went back without complaint to buy what she had forgotten to put on the list. His expressions of love through gifts were endearing: a meat block, a stainless kettle for cooking soups and sauces, and—my favorite—a dustpan with a long extended handle. Bending was no longer required to sweep up the dirt.

If it was Wednesday, Dad would sneak up behind Mom and gently slide his arms around her waist. Kissing her neck he would say, "Rosemary, you get more beautiful every day. Today you look like next Saturday." If it was Saturday, sometimes Mom and Dad fed us early, then—after we were in bed—shared a steak dinner by candlelight at our large oak kitchen table. On Sunday, he sat at one end of the church pew, with Mom at the other. Ted Bannon was proud of his 11 children who filled the space between.

No matter what day of the week it was, when it came time to say goodnight, he was there. One of my fondest memories is recalling the comfort that came in hearing the murmur of my parents' voices late at night. The house was quiet; I was supposed to be asleep. I didn't know what they were talking about, but as I rested upon my pillow, I felt as if I was listening to a lullaby. Their love for each other at the end of each day was my guarantee of a good night's sleep.

Dad loved to fish, reflecting an even disposition by the fact that it didn't matter if the fish were biting or not. He was an avid Cubs fan, which demonstrated his infinite patience and optimism. He looked adorable in blue jeans, handsome in a suit. My mother's photographs from his days in the Army prove he was a perfect example of why a woman loves a man in uniform.

Every Christmas morning as we stood at the top of the stairs in the hallway, Dad yelled to us from the living room, "Everybody go back to bed; Santa didn't show up." But he really did. Eleven equal stacks of gifts decorated the chairs lined up in front of our Christmas tree.

The only luxury my dad ever dreamed of was a brand new red Thunderbird. Never had one. Instead, he settled for "brand new" used station wagons. Occasionally, on hot summer nights, Dad and Mom took us to the Dairy Queen. After taking a head count, they ordered exactly enough nickel cones to satisfy themselves and the entire carload, the majority dressed in baby doll pajamas. My brother never had to get ready for bed before the outing and always got to sit in the front seat next to Mom. A long ride in the car cooled us off and settled us down as we headed back to the Bannon residence. The comforting sound of the wheels rumbling against the brick pavement on Armstrong Avenue assures me still that there is "no place like home."

I always felt safe. Never went hungry. If there were bills to pay but no cash to pay them, we never knew. Somehow the tuition was paid for 21 consecutive years for our education at a Catholic high school. Thankful for all he had, even more for what he did not, Dad was generous, loyal, and fair. In my eyes, my father never failed. He loved his wife more than himself, cherished his children, and believed without a doubt he was the richest man in town.

My mother gave birth 11 times between 1946 and 1963. She celebrated our lives as she created 11 birthday cakes a year, shaped like elephants, butterflies, and rocking horses. Carefully, she decorated them with boiled frosting, coconut, licorice, gumdrops, and Lifesavers. She never lost her focus as at least five little faces waiting to lick the bowl watched in anticipation, their 50 little fingers resting on the counter. Every birthday gift given was wrapped meticulously with coordinating paper and ribbon. Somehow she made sure none of us felt gypped, as if one child were more important than another. Each gift was as unique to the child as the child was to the gift-giver.

Hemming; tearing out hems; moving buttons, replacing them and finding those that almost matched consumed endless hours of her time. With discounted patterns and fabrics, Mom made corduroy Christmas jumpers, dotted Swiss and seersucker Easter dresses, graduation suits, prom dresses, and bridesmaid gowns. By the time Santa did show up in the living room, our dirty baby dolls had been made new with a little soap and water. They were clothed in new cotton sleepers and wrapped like newborns in soft flannel blankets, which just happened to match our new winter PJs.

We were the cutest Halloween devils in the neighborhood, with red food coloring spread evenly over the night cream Mom had smeared on our faces. I can feel the black eyebrow pencil pressing against my upper lip as Mom drew a mustache. Underneath my bottom lip she designed a goatee. As I raised my eyebrows, she said, "Look down, Honey," filling the natural hair line with exaggerated color. Old white sheets dyed with Rit #9 made the best jumpsuits and devil hats ever. She deserved an award for the patience she displayed while attaching badges to Brownie and Girl Scout sashes.

Mom allowed plenty of opportunity for fun. Ten daughters and one son meant birthday and slumber parties and celebrations for First Communions, Confirmations, and graduations. She never settled for white paper plates or sheet cakes from a local grocery store. Mom honored every accomplishment with a touch of class. In the process, her children learned to do the same, and her grandchildren receive the same royal treatment today.

She prepared well-balanced meals and packed healthy sack lunches; understood why we hated hot lunch on certain days and pleaded for it on others; encouraged us to eat dried prunes and apricots, and then surprised us with a Twinkie once in awhile. Mom's oatmeal was perfect every time. The hot chocolate she made from scratch was better than Steak'n'Shake's.

A shower and fresh makeup preceded her descent from the second floor to the kitchen every morning. She didn't go shopping with rollers in her hair. During the holidays, she always took us, two at a time, to see the magic behind the plate-glass windows in the department stores downtown. Those were the nights she treated us to burgers, fries, and shakes, or Chinese at a place called the Bamboo Inn. Everyone at home had—quick spaghetti.

Mom would never embarrass any of us in front of our friends. She taught us the fundamentals of good hygiene so we wouldn't be embarrassed. On school days as we squirmed through the last hour waiting for the bell to ring, she napped, reviving herself in preparation for our arrival home.

She talked on the phone when she wanted, as long as she wanted, because she was the mom. With a scratch of her fingernail, she found the best antiques under ten layers of paint. Every night she lit a candle at the dinner table in the spirit of prayer touched with a bit of romance. She met us in the bathroom at night if we threw up, wiped our faces with a cool washcloth, then tucked us back into bed. Every year we attended the mother/daughter banquet at St. Cecilia's. We were proud to be with her every time she won "the mother with the most daughters" award.

The three-story house on the corner was an eyesore the day the SOLD sign went up in the front yard. After many years of hard work, my parents turned it into our home. Not only did Mom strip the oak woodwork, she kept it looking magnificent year after year with the assistance of her daughters and Murphy's oil soap. Twice a year, 27 windows were washed with a concoction of water, ammonia, and vinegar, and then dried with crumpled pages of newspaper. Curtains were laundered, ironed with starch, then rehung; furniture pulled out and polished. She kept dresser drawers and closets organized.

Our attic became a treasure box filled with scrapbooks, yearbooks, and notebooks. First love letters and last ones. Dress-up clothes, baby doll clothes, Lincoln Logs, and baby doll body parts. First Communion veils, wedding veils, and photo albums. Science fair projects too inventive to incinerate, artwork too precious to pitch, and plaster handprints.

She began each day with the determination to nurture her family, sleeping like a rock at night because her perseverance had paid off. The diamond my father gave her on Christmas Eve 1944 was never replaced by anything bigger or more expensive. She embraced the commitment it represented. If she could have been granted one wish, it would have been a brand new red Thunderbird for my father.

My dreams were created because of these sweet memories. I am thankful to have been blessed abundantly by them. Most of my life I believed with all my heart that I would have a marriage strong and pure like my parents'. I yearned for a love like theirs. A love that lasted light years beyond a first glance. A commitment nurtured by holiness and grace.

Before my thirty-ninth birthday, I had survived one divorce and was hanging on by a thin thread trying to save my second marriage. My first divorce was right for me; my second almost destroyed me. Key word: almost. I am stronger, braver, wiser, and yes, thankful for every experience of my life.

I used to look at the statistics of my life as failure. Now I see that what I searched for most of my life has always been within me. It was not until I accepted responsibility for my poor choices, and forgave myself for all of them, that I began to understand what true love really is. God is love.

I wrote "The Place Is Here" at 2 a.m. on March 22, 1994, less than one month after my second marriage came to a devastating end. This song is a tribute to my faith. I believe now what I trusted then: Every burden eventually brings a blessing. My parents' marriage was faith in action, a model for what I wanted and needed. This song is dedicated to them.

There is a time for those in need,
To seek His face, to plant His seed.
There is a place where you can start to feel His love;
Just follow your heart.
The place is here, the time is now. Though your burden seems heavy,
He lifts it somehow.
Through His grace, compassion, and mercy, you'll find your way,
With the Lord.
Throughout the storm, He calms the water.
After the rain, He creates rainbows.
Sing a new song, then spread your wings.
Soar to the heavens. Trust in the Lord.

The place is here, the time is now. Though your burden seems heavy,
He lifts it somehow.

Through His grace, compassion, and mercy you'll find your way,
With the Lord.
You'll find your way.

Fall in love with the Lord.

Psalm 100

Shout for joy to the Lord, all the earth. Worship the Lord with gladness; come before Him with joyful songs. Know that the Lord is God. It is He who made us, and we are His; we are His people, the sheep of His pasture. Enter His gates with thanksgiving and His courts with praise; give thanks to Him and praise His name. For the Lord is good and His love endures forever; His faithfulness continues through all generations.

he brain is a little slow when it appears the world around you is crumbling. I traded my gaudy black Chevy van with mauve interior for a new teal Ford Tempo, saving myself over $100 a month in payments. When the salesman asked if I would like to purchase vanity license plates, I declined. Wait, I changed my mind. If a 12" x 6" piece of metal attached to the rear bumper of my car could be nominated for the "cheerleader of the century" award, ITLB OK would get my vote.

A lot of things changed in my life in 1994. One of my closest friends reminded me that she could only describe the entire situation by one comment: "The lights went out in your eyes." I have to admit, my spark had been extinguished.

I always believed these adages: God never closes a door without opening a window. There is a reason for everything. God never gives us more than we can handle. Yet, the circumstances surrounding the dissolution of my second marriage put my faith to the test. It was a test I never want to prepare for again.

This divorce prevented me from embracing some of the most powerful words from Ecclesiastes 3:1: "To everything there is a season, and a time for every purpose under heaven." Unfortunately, like many people who find themselves lost in despair, I was consumed by heartache, depression, and

exhaustion. Every hour, every day, I could not think beyond *my* loss, *my* pain. All the while, I was failing to recognize the ever-present gifts in my life—most importantly, my teenagers: Elaine, Kevin, and Maureen.

My valley of darkness became their burden as the role of motherhood was reversed. The greatest blessings of my life watched me lose my spirit. Strength, wisdom, and humor, displayed individually by my children, became my lifeline that year. As I recovered from what I believed at the time to be my life's greatest tragedy, these are some of the attributes and moments that saved me:

- Strength: Being my firstborn child, Elaine assumed responsibility for reminding me that life goes on. Missing her stepfather, she understood my sorrow. She encouraged me to practice what I preach: Accept that everything happens for a reason. Often, instead of going out with friends, she remained by my side, unselfishly comforting her mother.
- Wisdom: Kevin's arms wrapped around me as if I were his child; he patted my back over and over again. I sobbed on his shoulder as he said, "Mom, I want you to listen to me. It'll be OK. It's better than walking on eggshells." Ah, the practical new man of the house.
- Humor: On our first night alone, I let my black Lab outside and went to the basement to do laundry. Coming up the steps, I heard a noise and wondered, How did you get back in without my opening the door?

However, casting a huge shadow on the landing was a big, fat rat. It had escaped the cold, sneaking in the door when I let my dog out. It seemed bigger than me, moving faster than I could, finding refuge behind my kitchen stove. I was so numb from the events of that day, I let the dog in, turned off the lights and went upstairs.

Struggling with the confusion of their own emotions, my children were already in their bedrooms. Dreading the announcement, I shook my head. "Stay in bed. Don't go down to the kitchen. We have a rat in the house."

Maureen, who was 14 at the time, looked at me with red, swollen eyes. "Well, isn't that interesting: One rat walks out the front door in the morning and one sneaks in the back door tonight."

It is said "Time heals all wounds." The cliché proved itself in abundance. Through the encouragement of my children, I found hints of beauty in the spring and enjoyed a few carefree days during that summer. My heart was beginning to heal. I yearned for a way to renew my spirit.

The clock chimed. One, two, three. Three o'clock in the morning, still awake. Restless, I asked God to place a song in my heart. Just a simple tune, that's all I wanted. One encouraging hope, inspired by a dire need for peace.

With my guitar in hand, I retreated to the serenity of my favorite nook.

Sitting at my kitchen table, a soft breeze calmed me as it filtered through the screen of the open window. Two pewter candlesticks, holding red tapers, decorated the oak surface. I struck a match; fire and wick united to illuminate my place of refuge. As I focused on the beauty of the candlelight, my guitar became a stopping point for the tears that splashed upon its redwood and struck a chord in my heart.

Within moments I was inspired by the melody God had chosen for me. "Count Your Cookies" came as if racing to beat the first hint of sunlight that crisp autumn morning, destined to become my trademark song and the title of my fourth album. Paying the price for vanity plates paid off. ITLB OK.

Here's a little song I'd like to sing for you.

The words are sweet, the words hold true.

There are days that come along that will make you feel blue . . .

If you listen very closely, there's a lesson here for you.

I count my cookies, not my crumbs.

I don't count sheep, I count my miracles.

I count my blessings, not my burdens.

So, when life hands me a lemon, then I make some lemonade.

'Cause only I can make me happy, only I can make me smile,

Only I can tie my shoes so I can walk one more mile.

So, count your friends, not your foes.

When a baby's born, count his fingers and his toes.

That's a blessing, what a wonder.

So, if life gives you a lemon, you just make some lemonade.

'Cause only you can make you happy, only you can make you smile,

Only you can tie your shoes so you can walk one more mile.

I count my cookies, not my crumbs.

I don't count sheep, I count my miracles.

I count my blessings, not my burdens.

And when life hands me a lemon, I just make some lemonade.

'Cause only God can make you happy. Only God can make me smile.

He's the One to help me tie my shoes so I can walk,

He's the One to help you tie your shoes so you can walk,

He's the One to help us tie our shoes so we can walk

One more mile.

1 Timothy 4:4,5

For everything God created is good, and nothing is to be rejected if it is received with thanksgiving, because it is consecrated by the word of God in prayer.

ave you ever had a secret admirer? I did once . . . for about an hour. Hopeless romantics dream of moments like this. I had been singing most of the day. Upon returning to my office, I received a call from the flower room. "You've got flowers!" It was one of those unexpected delights. The kind that spurs curiosity and awakens sleeping endorphins. I scurried to pick up my surprise.

A fresh-cut garden bouquet packed the vase. "Oooh, Cook got flowers," was one comment I heard as I approached my office. "Meet someone special?" was another. I placed the arrangement on my desk and anxiously opened the card. In unfamiliar handwriting were two words: "Someday—Somehow."

My heart stood still. Did I sit back and revel in the moment? Oh no, not "little-miss-I-have-to-know-everything-right-now." Directly to the telephone I dashed and pondered with my sister-in-law, Lynn. "Who could it be?" "Why me?" "Do I know him?" "Do I want to know him?"

I had a split-second desire that Casanova was my high-school classmate, now a 42-year-old bachelor and one of my best friends. *Has he finally seen the light?* I thought, as my head did its best to confuse me. My heart, however, worked diligently to convince me of a fact I already knew:

His friendship was peerless. Crossing the boundary of our pact would surely lead to disaster.

My wishful thinking vanished faster than my enthusiastic endorphins had emerged, when another male friend came to mind. This guy was painfully recovering from a divorce. He was adorable, but surely not my soul mate. I dreaded hurting him in any way. The anticipation was too much. My solution: Call the florist.

Fast talking was critical in convincing the florist to disclose the patron's identity. With mission accomplished, I was disenchanted. I had no clue who this particular Romeo was. Never met him, didn't want to. So, I called my busybody sister-in-law again. This time, after disclosing his name, I asked her if she knew him. Of course, she did. "He's divorced, he has children, he's funny, he's cute, and gutsy."

I didn't care. My life was protected by an imaginary brick wall I had constructed around my previously broken heart. I was simply unwilling to give romance a chance, so the rebellious child in me had to come up with a solution to put a stop to such nonsense. I called the flower shop one more time, grateful to speak to a different clerk. I sent the same bouquet to him. My message read: "No Way—No How."

Big mistake! The guy was crushed, embarrassed, and angry. Guess who gave me that information? The busybody. She convinced me he was sincere and assured him I was worth pursuing. Once I realized how much I disappointed him by my response, I made every effort to fix it. We became friends in the process and he forgave me for being such a brat.

Another lesson learned: It never occurred to me the message delivered with those flowers was his way of saying, "I am interested in who you are. I admire what you do." I totally missed the point of such a rare gesture. My insecurity about relationships backfired due to my inconsiderate response. Everything may have been different had I been grateful for the beauty of the thrill of a secret admirer. But, timing is everything, as they say.

So, from the "Someday—Somehow" escapade came the title of this song. I actually wrote the refrain in the middle of the rain storm that I describe in the lyrics. I had gone on a walk because the skies and the spring air beckoned me. My clothes were drenched when I returned home that night. The story of the power of nature, as told in the song, was so fresh in my mind that I couldn't take the chance to become distracted. My guitar was more important than warm, dry clothes. A brisk walk that night gave birth to words that instilled in me courage, strength, and deepened faith. For me, time was about to stand still.

 The stars had settled in for the duration of the night.
I couldn't see the clouds as they were forming.
It seemed as if I'd never seen the moon shine so bright.
To my surprise, the rain came without warning.
But I continued down the street and picked up the pace.
Then I welcomed gentle rain upon my face.

Find joy in every trial and tribulation.
When you finally reach your destination,
You'll understand that every scar was worth the pain.
All you lost was a chance for gain.
That's when you'll find peace of mind.

And you'll cherish every breath.
Peace will gently touch your heart.

And your soul will be at rest.

The rain was hitting harder as I looked back on my life.
I remembered all the tears that I'd caused.
If I could change my foolish choices,
That pain cuts like a knife.
The thunder clapped so loud that's when I paused.
But I continued down the road, started to run.

A voice inside said, "Let it go, after rain
There's always sun."

Find joy in every trial and tribulation.
When you finally reach your destination,
You'll understand that every scar was worth the pain.
All you lost was a chance for gain.
That's when you'll find peace of mind.

And you'll cherish every breath.
Peace will gently touch your heart.
And your soul will be at rest.

The downpour couldn't stop me now; I could feel my pounding heart.
I was running so fast my body was burning.
Time will heal every wound; try to finish what you start.
Seize the day, cherish the moment; there's no turning.
The love you feel in your heart right now will find its way
Someday—Somehow.

Find joy in every trial and tribulation.
When you finally reach your destination,
You'll understand that every scar was worth the pain.
All you lost was a chance for gain.
That's when you'll find peace of mind.
And you'll cherish every breath.
Peace will gently touch your heart.
And your soul will be at rest.

Matthew 18:10,14

Take heed that ye despise not one of these little ones: for I say unto you, that in heaven their angels do always behold the face of my Father which is in heaven . . . Even so, it is not the will of your Father which is in heaven, that one of these little ones should perish.

eople often ask, "What do you find to be the most difficult aspect of your job?" Frequently, I answer their question with another: "What do you expect it would be?" "The death of a child" is their usual response. After years of serenading hospitalized children, I realize that faith is my beacon to understanding all aspects of childhood illness. Death included.

Preparing a beautiful nursery for my own babies brought me pleasure and great joy. Newly hung wallpaper reflected a child's playground, and I painted the woodwork the color of the morning sun. Resting upon the mattress of the oak Jenny Lind crib was the handmade quilt given to me by my best friend. The scent of Johnson's baby powder, lotion, and Dreft detergent permeated the room. The only thing missing was the new life I anxiously awaited. I imagine God waits patiently for the homecoming of all of his children.

Often when I have been present at the bedside of a dying child, I have pictured God Himself finishing the details of the little one's mansion. Everything is perfect; even the playground is complete. He blesses every room. Then blanketing the carousel with His spirit, He stands in awe, pleased with the work of His hands. It is time. He does not wait one more second for the child who

belongs to Him anyway. When death comes, I hold steadfast to all I believe, trusting heaven can only be improved by the jubilance of children frolicking there.

Child abuse is one facet that causes more upheaval throughout my daily endeavors than death itself. Along with the pediatrics staff, I was fond of a very angelic child. This thumb-sucking tyke had survived merciless abuse, faced death in the emergency room, became a warrior in pediatric intensive care, then eventually embraced the comfort and safety of our general pediatric unit.

The child was rarely alone. Sheltering arms of caregivers became a sanctuary over the weeks as the little one gradually recovered. Singing to the child every day was my honor. Everyone contributed to the cause, taking every opportunity to instill in this young patient a sense of security. Yet the sweetest security was obtained by the refugee's right thumb. Only breakfast, lunch, and dinner removed the thumb from its resting place. Otherwise, it seemed as if it was stuck behind a tooth or glued to the roof of the little mouth.

In the midst of my rounds one afternoon, I leaned over to focus my brown eyes upon the sleepy, aquamarine eyes of the patient. My coworker, Cindy, cradled the child, whose thumb was in its usual place and whose head, covered with soft golden locks, was resting upon her left shoulder.

Quietly, a little tune escaped my spirit, entwined with these lyrics. *"Could you tell me please what flavor is your thumb? Is it cherry? Is it chocolate?"* As Cindy chimed in, giggling and a little off key, *"Is it plum?"* With the inspiration of coworkers Chris, Theresa, Patsy, and Cindy, "The Thumb Song" was composed. It is dedicated to children of all ages who suffer the tragic injustice of abuse or neglect. Singing it becomes my prayer for the safety of children who are deprived of the right to a secure and loving environment. My faith reminds me: Do not condemn the enemy, but console and love the child. That's why I have refrained from revealing the gender of the child. I pray the childlike spirit of joy reflected in this song will remind each of us to protect, hold, and respect the children who bless our lives.

 Could you tell me please what flavor is your thumb?
Is it cherry? Is it chocolate? Is it plum?
You remind me of the days when I was three,
When my mama smiled and said these words to me:

"You could tell me if you pulled it out of there.
Why just one thumb when you know you've got a pair?
Is it stuck behind your tooth? Did you glue it to the roof?
Your thumb is one thing you don't have to share."

Could you tell me please what flavor is your thumb?
Is it cherry? Is it chocolate? Is it plum?

You remind me of the days when I was four,
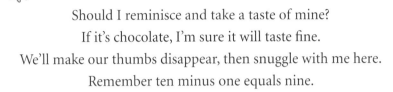
When my mama smiled and said: "I love you more."

Should I reminisce and take a taste of mine?
If it's chocolate, I'm sure it will taste fine.
We'll make our thumbs disappear, then snuggle with me here.
Remember ten minus one equals nine.

Could you tell me please what flavor is your thumb?
Is it cherry? Is it chocolate? Is it plum?
You remind me of the days when I was five,
And I knew that dreadful day would soon arrive.

So, goodbye to my thumb I finally bid.
I'm all grown up now, and I admit I did.
There's a simple purity to a child's security.
So, enjoy your thumb when you're a little kid.

Psalm 63: 1,3,6-8

God, you are my God. I search for You like someone in a dry, empty land where there is no water. Because Your life is better than life, I will praise You. I remember You while I am lying in bed; I think about You through the night. You are my help. Because of Your protection, I sing. I stay close to You; You support me with Your right hand.

ifteen years slipped through my fingers. Every dawn offered countless opportunities to perceive the elegance reflected through the innocence of the children I sang to every day. Each dusk reaffirmed my assurance that God is present in everything, that He is good all the time.

The gift that enables one to care for hospitalized children includes an inevitable roller-coaster ride: miracles, tragedies, illnesses conquered, and the heart-wrenching pain that comes with death uninvited. Taking care of "little heroes" is not a job, but a mission. The choice requires the ability to pass the torch at the end of each day.

The final year of the twentieth century, however, was difficult for me. As much as I wanted to believe I was spiritually and emotionally stable, my body rebelled, begging for rest. I suffered from lack of sleep. Even at rest, nightmares were my constant companion.

Securing a one-month sabbatical beginning Christmas Eve 1999, I was convinced it was time for a career change. My supervisor, coworkers, and friends begged to differ, believing I was born to sing in pediatrics, that I just needed some "Cookie time." There was quite an array of opinions from my very large family. Each person

held a deep concern, wanting more than anything for me to be content with my decision.

I sought an emotional, physical, and spiritual "rediscovery." Cravings such as these are not obtained by simple solutions. Guarded by my physician and guided by a professional counselor, I began to take better care of myself. Throughout the process, I was unaware that God was actually clearing my calendar, paving the road ahead for what was to come.

At their home in Florida, my sister Lorrie (daughter #7, child #8; charitable, soft-spoken, indecisive) and husband, Steve, provided a haven from winter in Peoria, Illinois, for my parents. I couldn't resist the invitation to contemplate my future under the warmth of the sun. Applauding my decision were my therapist, physician, and children.

On the second consecutive morning I had spent alone with my parents, we talked about the challenges restraining me. Growing up in a large family, I rarely had a private audience with them. So, believe me, at the age of 44 I was ready to appreciate this window of time, having Mom and Dad all to myself. That was one of the most intimate and healing encounters I had ever shared with the couple who devoted their lives to taking care of my ten siblings and me.

Combined with a heartfelt expression of respect and the desire to reconcile any of our differences, my parents set me free that 23rd day of January, with their unconditional love and wisdom. Blessed by their guidance, I gave myself permission to take the time I needed to reenergize.

After three hours of conversation and a pile of wet tissues, the tantalizing sunshine beckoned Dad and me to the back yard. He wore a short-sleeve yellow cotton shirt, faded blue jeans, and his Cubs hat that morning. A basket, nestled near his feet, contained about 20 oranges. I held the picker in my hand as my knees pressed gently against the steps of the aluminum ladder to maintain my balance. Cautiously, I reached for the bright orange spheres, pulling them from the branches one by one, passing them down to my father. The rustle of the tree and the snap of its branches consumed us as we became lost in our mission: fresh-squeezed orange juice.

Peering down from the ladder, I broke our silence. My father's Irish grin had captivated me. The question came with a curious intonation and a slight tilt of my head: "Dad, do you have any regrets?"

With a twinkle in his eye, he answered without hesitation: "I have one . . . I wish I would have married your mom the day after I met her."

I was not dumbfounded by his response. Dad loved Mom from the moment he met her, as she did him. On July 21, they would celebrate 55 years of marriage. So I tucked the moment into the scrapbook of my heart as we headed for the kitchen. Mom squeezed, and orange juice never tasted sweeter.

Early in February, the offspring of "Boss and Rosie" received a letter. Its contents were written by my sister Peggy (daughter #8, child #9; organized, creative, thoughtful), requesting that each of us write a story, poem, or prayer capturing any memories or treasured moments about Dad. Those very personal expressions of love would be given to him as a gift for his eightieth birthday on March 6, 2000.

Upon receiving the letter, my sister Terry (daughter #4, child #4; generous, lovely, a replica of our dad) called me: "I have a great idea! You have to write a song about Dad!"

Well, my guitar had been packed away in its hard-shell case since the night before Christmas eight weeks before. I had yet to hum a tune or strum a single note. My one-month leave had been extended; I had absolutely no intention of singing or playing my guitar again . . . ever. But the words my beloved father had spoken, while we were picking oranges, kept hovering in my heart. Suddenly I appreciated the challenge Terry had placed before me. How could I ignore the chance to boast about the artistry of my parents' love story in a song?

He was in uniform when he met her June 6, 1944, D-Day. A chance meeting over dinner at my grandmother's house in Parma, Ohio, sent my parents on a frenzy of trying to gather enough paper, envelopes, and stamps in order to correspond with each other. Today, that stationery is yellowed and fragile as it sleeps silently in the darkness of a cardboard box in my parents' attic. Yet those letters were filled with expressions of tenderness and an array of emotions. They were the means by which a solid family tree was to be created. Choosing faith as their soil, its roots would hold strong as God showered them with a united commitment to the sacrament of marriage. Our family tree sprouted many branches. Eleven children, 39 grandchildren, and five great-grandchildren (thus far) have reaped the benefits of the love that blossomed in the midst of the second world war.

Unlocking my guitar case, I wrapped my fingers around the neck of the instrument, reigniting a new passion for life. Pressing it against my heart, I felt a rush of thankfulness flood my spirit as if I were embracing my best friend. These words came as naturally as those of my father. *So I asked my daddy dear, do you have regrets at all? With a twinkle in his eye, he said, There's one I do recall. I should have stayed in Parma, when I knew I'd found my bride. I clearly loved your mama. My heart, it was my guide. When I laid my eyes upon her that sixth day of June, to marry her the seventh would not have been too soon.*

The afternoon of Boss's birthday, my family gathered in the living room at the home of my sister Kathy (daughter #2, child #2; pious, humble, reverant) as we honored the "Dad of the Hour." Two hours were saturated with laughter, the shedding of tears, unexpected moments of complete silence, and priceless performances (including the song I had written) by 11 of Boss's greatest fans. "One Regret" was the bridge that conquered an obstacle for me. It was the first of many "divine nudges" that eventually led me back to the bedside of my little heroes.

After returning home from Dad's birthday party, I reflected on the events of the weekend and its unforgettable memories. I felt at peace. I knew I was loved. Before I crawled into my bed, I treated myself to a glass of orange juice (not as good as Mom's) assured that God is good . . . all the time.

The train took him to Parma, a town just south of Cleveland;
His buddy Paul was seated by his side.
Without hesitation, the first time he saw Rosie
He knew he'd found a shelter in her eyes.
And in the midst of war that season, back in 1944,
My father found the woman . . . his heart was yearning for.

On the quiet eve of Christmas, she came to meet his family.
By the tree he placed a diamond on her hand.
She graciously replied, "I would love to be your bride."
She knew she'd found a treasure in this man.

So, I asked my daddy dear, "Do you have regrets at all?"
With a twinkle in his eye, he said. "There's one I do recall.
I should have stayed in Parma when I knew I'd found my bride
I clearly loved your mama, my heart, it was my guide.
When I laid my eyes upon her, that sixth day of June,
To marry her the seventh . . . would not have been too soon!"

The years brought many blessings, with daughter number one
They had three more girls, then they were blessed by their only son.
Tender love kept giving . . . there were six more little girls
Our home was filled with baby dolls, Lincoln logs and curls. . . .

So, I asked my daddy dear, "Do you have regrets at all?"
With a twinkle in his eye, he said. "There's one I do recall.
I should have stayed in Parma when I knew I'd found my bride
I clearly loved your mama, my heart it was my guide.
When I laid my eyes upon her, that sixth day of June,
To marry her the seventh . . . would not have been too soon!"

Now my daddy says he's rich, though he doesn't have much money.
He does not want power, fame or land.

He takes pride in knowing that his cup is overflowing.
It's all been given by the Father's hand.

So, I asked my daddy dear "Do you have regrets at all?"
With a teardrop in his eye he said, "Not one do I recall.
God took me to Parma so I could find my bride.
We've always loved each other; we stand still side by side.
When I see my ten daughters, my son, their children, and my wife,
I'm the richest man alive . . . I thank God for my life."
. . . I thank God for my daddy.

In loving memory of my father,
Edward "Ted" Bannon
March 6, 1920–March 24, 2002

 **1 Corinthians 2:9**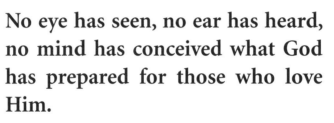

No eye has seen, no ear has heard,
no mind has conceived what God
has prepared for those who love
Him.

ith a somber heart and the phone to my ear, I listened as Karen explained the urgency of her request. "Michael is dying. The doctors don't know if he will live through the night. We've been taking turns holding him constantly for days. Rocking him, loving him, and keeping him as comfortable as we can. His brother, Nicholas, found a way to help me face the agony of losing him, bless his little heart. He told me, 'It would be cool if Michael had his own song so he can dance with Jesus when he goes to heaven.'"

My heart whispered to me . . . *If only grownups could understand heaven through the eyes of a child.* Karen continued, "I wrote a poem for Michael called 'Dancing With Jesus.' We know it's a lot to ask of you, but we want you to sing it for Michael's funeral. Only God knows when that will be, but even if it's in a few days, I know you can learn it. Your music has been a gift to us when Michael has been hospitalized. I'll have someone drop off the words for you at Children's Hospital. There isn't anyone else we want. You are in God's pathway today. He wants you to do this. For Michael."

Resting my left elbow upon my desk, I gently massaged my brow. Tears escaped my blurry eyes. Humbled by her strength and touched by her faith, I broke the silence. "I would be honored to sing your song at Michael's funeral. Choirs of angels will be singing for him. He won't need my music that day, but you will. I will come by the house after work so you can teach me the song. Do you have someone from your church to play the music on a keyboard, or is this a song you think I could play on my guitar? I might be able to play it if it's simple enough."

"Oh, Cookie, I only have the poem. I want you to write the music to go with it. I believe the melody will be given to you. It will be perfect for Michael's funeral. You are welcome to come here. I'll make a copy of the words. Please bring your guitar and sing for us while we rock Michael."

My calendar was clear for the next three days. Plenty of time to write a song. *A sign from Michael's dance partner*, I thought. I was on a mission for Michael as I made my way to his home. Of course, a concert for his siblings was a must, so I took my guitar as requested.

I entered their home. Love was plastered everywhere! Never in my life have I seen creativity displayed so proudly. It was like an art museum with free admission and a two-car garage. Works of art perfected with everything from watercolor paints and Crayolas to pencil and ink sketches. Karen's artistic abilities captured the little girl in me as I gazed awestruck at the Bible verses and murals on several large walls and soffets. Pictures created by little innocent hands were taped to walls from the front door all the way to the top of the stairs to Michael's little room at the end of the hall.

Peace to all who enter here, are the words that filtered within my soul when I crossed the threshold of his nursery. He was in the arms of a Sister from the Missionaries of Charity. It was apparent that she, like all who held Michael, had fallen in love. I envisioned the baby Jesus, as Karen gracefully, yet cautiously, lifted Michael and placed him in the shelter of my arms. My heart whispered, louder this time, *It won't be long Michael. Put on your dancing shoes, little one.* I knew God would put Michael's song in my heart. We laughed, we cried. Between giggles and tears, music filled the house and I left the gallery with a poem yearning for a melody.

Two weeks later, not a single chord complemented the expressions of love on the paper she had given me. Feeling under pressure, with great apprehension I called Karen. "I can't make this work. I think if I take your thoughts and put them in my words, they might flow with a tune I have in my mind. I can't believe Michael is still alive." *That's what happens when love takes charge.*

I could hear Karen smile as she said, "Whatever it takes, Cookie. Don't feel panicked; it will all come in God's time."

Michael had come to Jim and Karen through an answer to prayer. Seven years had passed since the death of their newborn son, Ryan. With three healthy children and unable to conceive another child, this young Catholic couple were united in their decision to pray. They selected a form of prayer called a novena.

Prayer comes in many forms. I become an intercessor when people ask me to pray for them. I say, "I will put you on my horizontal prayer list. That way, you remain at the top." I believe God hears, sees, and takes heed in granting that desire because it comes from my heart in faith. Our prayers are not always answered "our way," but God always answers them, providing us with all we need.

A novena is nine successive days of the same prayer offered to a selected religious figure, imploring that figure to intercede on one's behalf to our Father in heaven. Jim and Karen prayed a simple prayer, "For new life." They chose Mother Teresa as their intercessor. On the seventh day, they received a phone call. On the ninth day, they welcomed Michael into their home.

When Michael's 14-year-old mother went into labor, no one else knew she was pregnant. How abandoned she must have felt. New life and extreme pain conquered her fear as she admitted herself to the emergency room, complaining of an appendicitis. An emergency Caesarean section brought Michael into the world. However, after six hours trapped within the birth canal, a bleak outcome was inevitable.

Certain this baby would not survive, authorities began the process of placing him in a state-run facility. For two weeks, physicians and nurses cared for him as social service considered the possibility of a temporary home. As Jim and Karen began the seventh day of their novena, God answered their simple prayer, "For new life." On the ninth day, they saw Michael as he had been created. Beautiful, precious, and irresistible. To the amazement of hospital personnel,

Jim declared with finality, "Pack his bags, we're taking him home. I'm sold on this child. You say we're not connected in any way, but faith has connected us, and God knocked loudly."

It was six weeks before the family realized the severity of his problems. Nothing startled Michael. He could not see. He could not hear. His siblings communicated with him by dancing around his infant seat. The vibrations were so powerful their baby brother could not resist a smile. With love like that, they were sure he felt it in his heart. When Karen called with her request, 21 months surrounded by pure, unconditional love had blessed this family.

Karen's encouragement to "Do whatever it takes" allowed the song in my heart to blend like a symphony with the words to the poem, "Dancing With Jesus." When I completed the music to every stanza, I called Karen, delighted that our mission had been accomplished. The following morning, I entered their household, guitar in hand, and sang Michael's song to the family. At four o'clock that afternoon, Michael was given his dancing shoes. It wasn't Karen who gave me enough time to write the song for Michael's funeral. It was God.

The kids are in the living room, doing their show again.
The music booms as they perform.
Their brother sits in silence; he's the fan they all prefer.
What he can't see, he can't hear, he feels with his heart they're sure.
Michael's been a fighter since the day he arrived;
The doctors had assured us he could not survive.
The twinkle in his eyes, only God knows.
So our cup of love and gratitude overflows.
There's no need to worry about what Michael cannot see;
We don't cry over what he'll never be.
We take each day as a miracle, chasing away the doom,
Michael will be dancing in heaven with Jesus soon.

Michael has worked miracles in simple ways;
His wondrous smile sings God's awesome praise.
If you wonder, is there purpose in his birth,
You've not been blessed by what he teaches, his worth.
Thank you, Michael, for bringing light to each day.
The angels wrote your music; they'll show you the way
To kick up your heels and see with your eyes.
Dance with all your might;
Dancing will fill eternity once Jesus is in your sight.
Run swiftly, Michael, Jesus will lead you home;

He is waiting for you on His golden throne.
You'll suffer no more, you'll cry no more tears.
Eternity we will share.
Dance, Michael, dance, with Jesus dance.
Dance, Michael, dance, we'll meet you there.

In memory of Michael

Matthew 11:28-30

Come to me, all of you who are tired and have heavy loads, and I will give you rest. Accept my teachings and learn from me, because I am gentle and humble in spirit, and you will find rest for your lives. The teaching that I ask you to accept is easy; the load I give you to carry is light.

he melody filtered about in my mind and fluttered within the hollow of my heart for several years. Adapting it to best serve my surroundings sufficed for awhile, yet its simplicity yearned for a title. I was sure that when I least expected, the moment would arrive when one little soul would become the song's namesake. Irresistible faces embellished by brilliant eyes and breathtaking grins were my audience for numerous rehearsals that prepared me to meet the flawless champion who would claim the territory.

His name was Jack. Our meeting came as a soft summer rain, decorated by a hint of sweet blue sky, salt-and-pepper clouds and the magic of a rainbow. Jack is a heart magnet. A child truly created in the image and likeness of God. Perfect in the eyes of his maker, blessed by two of life's greatest gifts: unconditional love and perseverance.

Imagine this little boy, cradled in the shelter of his mother's arms, his head limp against the crevice of her elbow. Denied the thrill of bouncing up and down upon her knee, drained of the energy it takes to wrap his little fists around her index fingers so he can stand like a big boy on his mama's thighs, as she pulls him up slowly. His life disrupted by an uncontrollable seizure disorder.

This cherub captured me with his transparent blue eyes and silken red hair as he began his inordinate mission to rearrange my heart. Apparently, he had succeeded in this area—of hearts, I mean. It was evident by the way his mother looked at him that he had already stolen hers.

She appeared quite cozy, dressed in a white T-shirt and a pair of soft cotton pajama pants. No shoes, only socks blanketed her feet. Even the windowsill contained some comforts of home: hot coffee and a large bag of M&Ms. A cobalt blue chair, draped with pillows and blankets, served as her temporary bed.

The ashen color of her skin and her vacant eyes reflected the contrary. She was engrossed only in the well-being of her afflicted child, and her heart revealed itself through her somber smile. She welcomed the opportunity for Jack to experience his first "live Cookie concert" as I began to sing. I strummed. I sang. I wept, watching seizure upon seizure after seizure, one following another with little or no rest in between.

The motherly love Kris portrayed was reminiscent of my mother's when my sister Maureen (daughter #1, child #1; independent, liberated, spiritual) broke three vertebrae in a tobogganing accident during her freshman year of nursing training in 1965. Mom transformed the dining room into a temporary bedroom. With ten other children at home, the youngest at age two, Mom cared for Maureen as if she were her only child. Being loved with so much conviction is a gift.

In that same gentle way, Kris comforted Jack, her only child, until the taut muscles of his fragile body released themselves from the invisible demon. "It'll be all right, Jack. I'm here, Jack. Mommy is here," she whispered. Tears welled up in my eyes. Mesmerized by the moment, I sensed this was the dawn of another "love affair" in my life. The journey has included many, with those people less than four feet tall captivating me one heartstring at a time.

So, Jack's song became a tradition at his bedside with every hospitalization. The first few lines remained the same, but no one, including me, ever knew what surprise would come with a verse. Anything and everything about his family, our pediatric staff, and eventually plans for our future together, created the context that ultimately resulted in a finished ditty dedicated to Jack.

"Oh, Jack, would you please marry me?" melted the burdened and broken hearts of Jack's parents and grandparents time after time, as the little tune carried Jack from seizure to seizure. Then God, in His infinite mercy, would allow just enough time in between for an unforgettable smile that literally moved my heart from "here to over there."

You're the cutest little thing that I ever did see;
Oh Jack, how I wish you belonged to me.
I know your mom and daddy would never let me take you home.
You've got the sweetest blue eyes; I love your red hair.
You make my heart jump from here to over there.
Jack, when I'm with you I never feel alone.

'Cause you're the sun in disguise when you are smiling at me;
The moon on the rise with the spirit so free.
Not a star in the sky can shine quite like you do . . .
And you're only two.

Oh Jack, would you please marry me?
I'll wait all my life, Jack, you'll see.
Take your time, think it through, I know I sound bold.
What's that you say, Jack? You have an answer for me?
"Not today, not next week, not next year when I'm three!
You know I adore you, your songs are sweeter than gold . . .
But, Cook, you're too old!"

You're still the thrill of the tide when it's touchin' my toes;
The sweetness of snow on the tip of my nose.
Not a bird in the sky can spread his wings like you do.
Oh, Jack, I love you. I really do.

God bless you Jack.

Isaiah 40:30-31

Even children become tired and need to rest, and young people trip and fall. But the people who trust the Lord will become strong again. They will rise up as an eagle in the sky; they will run and not need rest; they will walk and not become tired.

orn May 6, 1978. Four weeks premature, weighing 7 pounds and 4 ounces. Lungs and liver not yet developed, at risk, and 17 days in neonatal intensive care.

He was all boy. Basketball, baseball, soccer. Several stitches, black eyes, some broken bones due to his energetic personality. Mischievous throughout grade school, typical detentions in high school. Should have been grounded more. Not interested in college, found a job instead. Moved out. Bummed around with his buddies. Too much rent. Not enough cash. There's no place like home.

The schemes of adolescent guys. Discovering the ebb and flow of poor choices, then suffering the consequences. A minor incident leads to serving community hours. Ironically, while walking home after completing his punishment, he feels the pressure of a sharp object against his lower back. A mugger steals his wallet. Badly shaken, he slowly walks away, peering over his shoulder, thankful a blade didn't penetrate him.

Things are "looking up." Finds a job he enjoys. Skilled at the grill. Meticulous like his mother. Keeps his work area spotless. Begins to show some responsibility. Mom is hopeful, trusting. Seems almost too good to be true. Then, a disrupting phone call. One night off. Too much fun leads to a new debt to society. A serious lesson learned.

Continues to put his heart and soul into work. Pays Mom a little rent. Heads down the right track. 11 p.m., time to close the restaurant. He becomes a victim of a robbery. Forced to his knees, he follows orders to unlock the safe. His life flashes like a meteor before him as the pressure of a pistol groping his neck terrorizes him. The gunman runs away a lot richer, out of sight, not out of mind. Recalling the crime causes him to shudder. Reliving the experience is too much to take.

Different restaurant. New surroundings. Safer neighborhood. Appreciated by a boss who becomes his mentor, who happens to be his uncle. Leadership skills begin to sink in: a "right-hand man" blossoms. Fewer gatherings with the guys. A sweet girlfriend, a little golf at dawn. Blue eyes that melt your heart, yellow roses on the kitchen counter for his mother. The Post-It note pressed against the vase reads: To my #1 Valentine.

Insurance bill arrives on July 14, 2000. Car insurance lapsed. Mom robs mortgage insurance stash to pay his debt. Frustrated, she angrily calls him at work. "You owe me a lot of money." That week he works overtime.

Two days later, he waits at a stoplight with Mama. Children and adults approach a large church on the corner. His remark disturbs her. "This traffic is ridiculous on Sunday morning. These people drive me crazy. They're all hypocrites pretending to be Christians because it's Sunday."

The passenger states her case, "Zip your lip. Be careful what you say about Presbyterians, Lutherans, Baptists, Catholics, or anyone who is part of a community of believers. We are all hypocrites. There is only one God. I assure you, when your life is in the deepest trouble you have ever faced, these are the people who will pray you back to life!"

Four days pass. July 20, 2000. The telephone rings at 4:19 a.m. An unfamiliar voice asks, "Are you the mother of Kevin West?"

My left hand crushes the mattress. With an increased heart rate I quickly sit on the edge of my bed. "Kevin is my son."

A single-car accident. Des Moines, Iowa. Four-and-a-half hours from home. No fatalities. Kevin was driving without a seatbelt. The two passengers involved are Kevin's good friends. One treated and released, the other admitted to intensive care but is in stable condition. "The trauma surgeon is waiting to speak with you about the condition of your son. Please hold."

Dead at the scene. Revived by medical helicopter service. Intubated in a field. Critical condition. Intensive care. Closed-head injury. Comatose. "He may never wake up. If he does, he may not know you." Ventilator. Spinal cord injury. Quadriplegic. "Your son will never walk again . . . if he survives."

Prayer. Shock, fear, chaos, more prayer. Tears. Uncontrollable shaking. Heartache. Grief. Awakened by the phone call, my daughter Maureen embraces me in the kitchen. We tremble in each other's arms. Questions unanswered.

A peaceful night camouflaged by calamity. A son. A sibling. A hero. Pain. Uncertainty. Unbearable agony.

A series of many phone calls begins at 4:30 a.m. The first, to my sister Ginny, a registered nurse. Noble, calm, focused. Listens without interruption. By my side before 5 a.m. She calls the hospital for an update. Overcome with sadness, she remains strong as she is informed of the details. With extraordinary compassion, she urges me to consider these possibilities: Death. Organ donation. Life given as a gift. A funeral home. "I know you've been with families facing these decisions so many times. It's different now, with your own child. You have more strength than you realize. Do you think you can do this?"

With conviction, I reply, "Yes."

Only steps behind, my sister-in-law Lynn anchors herself next to me. Loyal, diligent, protective. Blessed with the gift to create a morsel of joy when sorrow does its best to destroy it, she reminds me of what a fighter Kevin is. Tears are streaming down her face and her bottom lip is quivering. "He fought for his life the day he was born, he'll do it again today." Immediately she organizes plans to send my daughters and me to Kevin's bedside via the airlines.

Then, my married daughter Elaine stands immobile before me near the back door of the kitchen on the landing. Three steps up to the kitchen, eight steps down to her little brother's room in the basement. Our swollen eyes meet. The sting of life subsides for a moment as we cradle each other.

Maureen burrows between us. Our family is missing the one who causes the most havoc. We love him anyway. It feels as if our world has crumbled into a million fragments.

An overnight bag. If he dies, I won't need this. My guitar. Just in case. I walk down the stairs to Kevin's room, aware of my ability to do so, realizing he will never do this again. I smell his pillow, leave his dirty cereal bowl and spoon on the coffee table, then feed his fish. Touching his golf clubs, my chest feels crushed as I remember blowing him a kiss from the doorway 22 hours ago. I fear he will die before I have a chance to say, "I love you, Kev." Daylight leisurely embarks upon me as I lock my back door. The rescue has begun.

Two chauffeurs. Three airline tickets. Bloomington to Des Moines. 7:11 a.m. flight. We arrive 13 minutes before takeoff. Two minutes too late. The doors have been shut. No exceptions. FAA regulations. Back to Peoria. Ninety minutes wasted. Plan B.

My only brother, my son's namesake, assumes the responsibility of driving five passengers to his nephew's bedside. Cautiously, as if he has been given temporary wings, he heads west toward Iowa. With faith abounding, he requests that his spouse call the local Christian radio station. Another link to an endless prayer chain.

On any other day in July, I would have been consumed by the lush green cornfields along that Illinois highway. But that early summer morning slipped away as my conversation with the trauma surgeon echoed within my mind. By the time I would pass that way again, those fields, packed with countless stalks of hearty grain, would display a stark empty blanket of shredded husks embedded in the same soil that provided its life.

Reality emerges. Fear and anxiety cascade upon me. I am numb. This can't be happening. I am lost by what is within me. *Will he live? Will he die? Death. Organ donation. Life given as a gift. A funeral home. Will God call him home? Will God let me take him home? My home without ramps. My home with them.* Although I pray, I don't know what to pray for.

My humanness, my selfishness, directs my prayer toward begging God to let him die. *This cross is too heavy for me to carry. I don't want the possibility of caring for my grown disabled child. Comatose. Unable to communicate. Head injury. Frustration. Ventilator. Caregivers. He is only 22.* I believe I know my son better than God does. Thoughts ricochet in my head. *He will hate them for saving him. He will hate me for letting them. He will hate his wheelchair. He will despise his life. Will I despise his life? I am ashamed of my doubt. I want to believe. I want to believe ITLB OK.* Then, as if slapped by the wings of a very insightful angel, I drastically shift the direction of my prayer.

Recalling the previous Sunday morning sends me into a tailspin. Stoplight. Church on the corner. Hypocrites. He is in the deepest trouble he has ever faced. His hour has come. The prayer chain is endless. He didn't know God last

Sunday. Fear of his destiny and my desire for him to know Christ redirect my petition. Grace. At its finest.

Serenity settled within me. I vowed to leave Kevin at the foot of the cross. My tears fell like rain, as they should; yet I trusted God and God alone. I believed. I trusted He would lift my little one from the eye of the storm. At that moment, I knew that God would be in every port. Now, my only purpose was to be Mom.

I arrive at Kevin's bedside at 12:06 p.m. Ginny grasps my hand as we enter room 11 in the intensive care unit. Recognizing my son is almost impossible. Spinal shock. Life support. Five hundred stitches in his left eye. Tubes, needles, lacerations, broken bones, IVs, transfusions. I watch what happens around me. I speak silently. *Kev, I'm here. Do you know who I am? Do you know who you are? Where can you feel me touch you? Are you in pain?* I touch his face gently. I know he knows I am with him. Tears trickle beyond his temple. I kiss them away. His sky blue eyes open.

Six days sustained by a ventilator. A spinal fusion. Thirteen weeks in a halo. Five weeks in Des Moines. Being fed by your mother again. Neuro-intermediate care. Plastic surgery on the left eye. Fevers. Hallucinations. Catheters. Blood clots in his lung and his leg. Problems with Coumadin. Severe reaction to Heparin. Gushing blood. Transfer to ICU. More transfusions. Packed cells. Plasma. Another obstacle overcome. A remarkable staff. A favorite housekeeper, Ben, sings reggae a cappella every day. Temporary pain relieved through a song.

Music is contagious. A blessing in disguise. Kevin makes us laugh until we cry as he sings "Come Sail Away" in the voice of Cartman from *South Park*. Time to close the door to his room, aware of patients who may be sleeping. A welcomed diversion.

Stacks of mail. A gift bag to hold them. Letters of encouragement and cards filled with hope keep coming. A trip to Wal*Mart for a large plastic container. Family, friends, coworkers, former patients, strangers. Checks, cash, phone cards, countless anonymous donations. Acts of love from across the miles that comforted us during some very dark days. ITLB OK.

A nerve-racking flight to Chicago. The Rehabilitation Institute. Challenges defeated. Sponge baths are history. The exhilaration of a first shower. Refusal to use a motorized chair. Exposed to what could have been. A favorite patient. An inspiration to others. The blessing of being thankful. An amazing ability to grieve. He never complained. The day he said "Mom, I love you more than myself," I cried.

His affection was short-lived however. Exhausted from lack of sleep, I finally sat down for a nap one afternoon. Kevin asked me to rub his shoulder. Frustrated, I released a huge sigh, prompting his snide remark: "Well, if it's not the 'Queen of Sighs.'" Feeling no shame, I stood up, walked out, and enjoyed the thrills of Michigan Avenue for three hours. He apologized.

Bargaining is not an option with God. He doesn't cut deals or hand out incentives. It was not my "promise" to leave Kevin at the foot of the cross, but only the infinite mercy of God that rescued my son in every circumstance. When fear summoned me, I retaliated with a prayer of conviction. *I gave birth to Kevin. God gave him life. I am his mother; God is his Savior. The foot of the cross; leave him there; don't take him back.* I never did.

My gift of music carries me to the bedside of children who, along with their families, embrace the challenges of tragedy. Eighteen years of my life had been devoted to a cause: sharing a part of myself through the simplicity of a song, hoping to create a moment of peace, to lessen the anxiety of an unexpected or unwanted situation. The morning of July 20, 2000, God lifted me up, surrounded me with love, then—keeping His promise as the great "I Am"—He gently carried me to the other side of the bed.

As the days of my life unfolded, never did I believe that I was immune to a catastrophe within my own family. Few escape the devastation of its intrusion, yet through faith, many transform it to triumph. In the blink of an eye, I went from servant to being served. Nothing has humbled me as much. With each obstacle balanced by a miracle, the minutes became hours. Surpassing every barricade, we approached a new dawn as the days transformed into months of healing.

On Christmas Eve 1999, when I packed my guitar into the darkness of its hard-shell case, I believed with all my heart that my singing career had ended, unaware God was preparing me for that early-morning phone call on July 20.

After seven months of intense counseling, I was rested, refreshed, and ready to return to work on July 30. My PTO time was gone, short-term disability exhausted. Ten days away from going back to work, the plans changed. I was needed at the bedside of a very special child: my only son.

My family traveled two by two, as if exchanging a torch fed by the fire of love. Within a week, my friends and coworkers gave me more than five hundred hours of their personal vacation time. It was their love and generosity that allowed me to stay with Kevin for seven weeks until he was ready to face his rehab program alone. I came home for the first time September 8. Seeing Chicago in the rearview mirror and leaving Kevin after 50 days was bittersweet, but necessary.

The time had come for me to find a way to make my home wheelchair-accessible. My humble little abode couldn't be our home anymore. The search was draining, and every "For Sale" sign ended up a dead end. But then as quickly as I gave up my address, God Himself had chosen a new one.

I met Dave and Sandy in August 1986, when their daughters, Michelle, 16, and Nicole, 14, were involved in a tragic car accident. Nicole recovered; Michelle died from severe head injuries. When I met Sandy, I immediately recognized Jesus in her eyes. Her husband resembled His presence also. I helped them plan Michelle's funeral service in the midst of their devastating loss. I sang for the Mass, and as her classmates placed roses on the altar, I sang

"Friends," the first song I had ever written. Dave and Sandy have been angels in my life ever since.

On September 23, they convinced me to take a look at a wheelchair-accessible home that had been on the market for almost two years. Everything was there: ramps, wide doorways, and even a roll-in shower. We were there less than 15 minutes when Dave wrapped his arms around me and said, "Finally, after all these years, we can give something back to you. You were there for us when we lost Michelle. You, Kev, and Mo are going to live here. I don't care if we have to remortgage our own home to make it happen. When Kevin leaves Chicago in November, this is the place he will call home." The events following that conversation were completely orchestrated by God.

From that moment on, it was out of my hands. Dave and Sandy, along with four of my dearest friends, formed a "Fill the Cookie Jar" committee. Plans for a fund-raiser were in action in less than two days. A local bank, with a president whose heart was guided by blind faith, gave me a six-month bridge loan with no down payment and God as my cosigner. Learning to receive has been one of the sweetest lessons of my life.

On October 9, the loan officer handed me the keys after I signed my name on the dotted line. Literally, for 37 days and nights, angels—tall, short, strong, creative, quiet, silly, talkative, and sometimes even invisible—worked without tire. Every room scrubbed and painted. New flooring for easy rolling. Windows replaced and even washed to let the "Son" shine in. It was Jesus with everything from a paintbrush to a pan of lasagna. Jesus with work gloves, overalls, hammers, and He even threw in a stepping stone for the yard, with these words painted around the edges: "For everything there is a season, a time for every purpose under heaven."

I was awakened by a sound at 3 a.m. on November 4. An incredible sense of awe in my heart led me to the realization that I was unable to repay the universe for all of the blessings given me. I needed to give back. Embracing my guitar, welcoming the stillness of the night, I wrote "Every Day." My song of praise thanks God for his countless acts of love and for saving my son.

Gifted with a spirit for life and the ability to see beyond the barrier of loss, Kevin was and remains thankful. In my eyes, he's my little boy, who along an unexpected pathway had become a man. I smile recalling Kevin's comments about the top three reasons to be paralyzed:

#1. Anytime you go anywhere in a wheelchair, somebody asks "Can I help you? Do you need something? Is there anything I can get for you?"

#2. You always get to ride shotgun!

#3. I never have to say, "Does my butt look fat in these pants?"

On the evening of November 15, 2000, my son pushed himself through the doorway of our home, a place he had never seen. It was a sanctuary provided for us by a miraculous community of countless gift-givers, some within reach, many unseen. St. Francis of Assisi said, "It is in giving that we receive." It has been almost impossible for me to take my feelings of sincere gratitude from my heart to my hand. My life has been blessed abundantly. With a spirit of charity, not a detail left undone, an empty house was molded into a home blessed by the hands of selflessness. There are no words big enough in the dictionary to express my thanks to those who spread their wings and folded their hands for us . . . You know who you are. May God bless you . . . abundantly.

From the moment I heard of his pain,
I prayed, Lord, You'd welcome him home.
I feared, Lord, "What would he gain?"
He believed he could make it through his life on his own.
So, I prayed, Lord, ignore my prayer—give me strength to be there.
Save his life, Lord, please find a way.

Every day You lift me up with Your angels;
Every night You bring me to my knees.
Every prayer has been answered because of Your power;
Not a detail left undone.
Every day, Lord, I thank You for saving my son.

The moment I saw his blue eyes,
My tears fell upon him like rain.
Those I love gathered close by my side.
The rescue began to ease all the pain.
The peace that suspended me
Once I surrendered his life into Your hands;
I was blessed by the joy as I watched my
Little boy become a man.

Though his legs will not move, he can race.
His future to some might seem small.
I believe there's a time and a place
For those to get up when they fall.

From the moment You heard of my pain,
You showered my life with surprise.
When it seemed all was lost, You remained.
New scars always open our eyes.

I praise You for being right there.
Thank you, God, for ignoring my prayer.

Every battle we face will be won,
Because of Your Son.
Every day You lift me up with Your angels;
Every night You bring me to my knees.
Every prayer has been answered because of Your power;
Not a detail left undone.
Every day, Lord, I thank You.
Every night, Lord, I praise You.
Every day, Lord, I thank You
For saving my little one . . .
For saving my son.